Scab

A Comic Drama
in Two Acts

by Sheila Callaghan

SAMUEL FRENCH

FOUNDED 1830

NEW YORK HOLLYWOOD LONDON TORONTO

SAMUELFRENCH.COM

ISBN 978-0-573-69671-8   Printed in U.S.A.   #29080

MUSIC NOTE

IMPORTANT BILLING AND CREDIT
REQUIREMENTS

PRODUCTION HISTORY

Women's Expressive Theatre, New York City, 2002.

Eternal Spiral Productions, Philadelphia, Pennsylvania, 2003.

Impact Theatre, Berkley, California, 2003.

The Blue House Theatre, Los Angeles, California, 2004.

CHARACTERS

ANIMA – 23 year-old woman

CHRISTA – 22 year-old woman

JENNA / ANGEL ONE – 20s-30s woman

ALAN / ARTIE / DAVIE / ANGEL TWO – 32 year-old man

MOM / KELLEE / MARY-ANDROGYNE – 40s woman

SPECIAL THANKS

Patricia Tilburg, Bryan Davidson, John A. Callaghan, Kristin Ohrt, Rhea Seehorn, Mia Barron, Elizabeth Reaser, Erin Gann, Joseph Murphy, Colleen Quinlan, Playwright's Horizons, Tim Sanford, Sonya Sobieski, Deron Bos, Hilary Ketchum, Kip Fagan, Dorothy Lemoult, Printer's Devil Theatre, Flora Diaz, Victoria Pettibone, Sasha Eden, Shannon Burkett, Anne Carney, David Wheir, Hayley Finn, John Kaufman, Tricia Rodley, Jerry Patch, Olivia Honeggar, and South Coast Repertory Theater

MOVEMENT ONE

(A phone rings thrice in the blackness. Lights full on **ANIMA** *in the apartment, lying sideways on the floor and wheezing. A large bucket of dead wildflowers festers in the corner and a beat-up second-hand sofa lingers crookedly in the center of the room. Slats of morning light blanche the floor and Anima's rumpled clothing, which appears not to have been changed for days. There is a knock.)*

CHRISTA. *(offstage)* Hello?

(Another knock. **CHRISTA** *enters with her suitcase.)*

CHRISTA. My goodness you're on the floor well I'm here it took me long enough it's a five hour flight the bus system here is appalling is that my room?

*(***CHRISTA*** *steps over* **ANIMA** *and exits.* **ANIMA** *wheezes.)*

(The slats of light creak across the floor and it is now afternoon. **CHRISTA** *re-enters the room with her camcorder poised at her eye.)*

CHRISTA. Wow, you're still on the floor well I have nothing to do until my meeting at seven with my new classmates over coffee how grad school of us I'm going to check out the neighborhood right now you have an interesting place or should I say we

*(***CHRISTA*** *aims the camcorder lens at her face.)*

Well here's my new apartment and there's my new roommate on the floor and here's my first day in Los Freaking Angeles

(She exits.)

(Lights move again and fade to a blue shade of evening. **ANIMA** *is still on the floor.* **CHRISTA** *enters holding a white deli bag.)*

CHRISTA. There you are again, ha, do you ever get up to pee, boy I'm exhausted I already have seminar tomorrow my cohorts are geniuses they all came from ivy leagues I can't finish this sandwich if you want it jesus christ will you just look at me

(**ANIMA** *does not move.* **CHRISTA** *kneels on the floor next to* **ANIMA**.)

CHRISTA. It always helps me to verbalize when I'm miserable

(**CHRISTA** *touches* **ANIMA**, *who jerks violently.*)

I have to prepare for this thing

(**CHRISTA** *exits.*)

ANIMA. This is it:

It was the third one that did it at three thirty in the morning in the night or the night/morning that no one can seem to make up their mind about which is it really, not even the sky that stays dark until it's damn good and ready to lighten up even when you are not.

The third ring that shot me out of bed and for no apparent reason made me feel urgency. Not fear urgency. It was like I remembered a pot of boiling water on the stove that was spilling over and wetting the pilot light that for some reason didn't go out when it got wet.

The ring, the ring. I leaped up and I was naked and as I ran to the phone I felt the cellulite of my ass bounce a little and I involuntarily sucked in my gut because that is what I have learned to do now when I am naked or in a bikini or ashamed of the little womanly curve above my pubic bone that was sexy on Marilyn Monroe. And my breasts that are round and lovely in my wonderbra but point out to either side like the eyes in the head of a lizard were doing just that as I ran to the phone the phone the phone

Ring and I picked it up and my eyes were wide in the dark and I saw colors, the black was segmented into photograph pixels like a color shot in a magazine, the grainy kind like in Paris Match not the glossy super

American high fashion perfection of Vogue or Vogue or that other Vogue/Cosmo/Teen nonsense. The black gets divided in colored pixels at night now and then ever since I did acid my sophomore year in college in that wonderfully large cathedral club in new york where everything was frightening and hysterical and put there for my entertainment and not real. not real.

My hand on the phone. My elbow touching the coiled cord as the phone was lifted to my ear. My arm was naked, the cord was cold. Coiled. Cold coiled cord and I said oh God I said why did I say it I said could I really have said it but I said. Hello.

(**ARTIE** *steps into the light, holding the phone.*)

ARTIE. Annie. It's Artie. Daddy died this morning.

ANIMA. Oh. Can you call me back?

(**ARTIE** *disappears.*)

I must have hung up the phone because it rang later, not five but seven, twenty, a hundred years later that night again but I don't remember placing the receiver back down. I remember my inner skin being cold and my outer skin being hot and I walked in to my room and picked up my shirt and pulled it over my head but Funny. I can't recall if I told Him before or after I put my shirt on.

(**ALAN** *steps into the light, sleepy and naked and wearing a sheet.*)

He had heard the Ring Ring and Ring as well but it meant little to him because HIS phone sounds different than MINE so the mental alarm that goes off when your phone rings very late/early didn't go off for him so he was unprepared for what. I. Said.

(**ALAN** *is shocked and sympathetic-looking.*)

He was skinny and naked and nine years older than me and suddenly I couldn't see him. I saw an outline of who I thought he was, but his center had just dripped out right before my very eyes ladiesandgentlemen

ALAN. Oh Annie I'm so sorry

ANIMA. This skinny naked needle of a man whom I
respected because he was in my field and better, I
thought, than me but maybe not maybe just different
but I thought better, in my grad program and here he
was NAKED shhh don't tell anyone big secret hee hee
we're fucking, don't you know, yep what fun

(**ALAN** *reaches out to hug* **ANIMA**.)

don't

No embrace, please, no arms, there's something not
right about all this and I don't really need to be con-
soled I just have to figure it out. Give me a second.
Give me five minutes. Ten years. I've got time.

(**ALAN** *disappears. The phone rings.*)

ANIMA. Artie, again. Paramedics, dogs barking, grandma
crying, Mom did CPR because she's a nurse how is
Mom finefinefine, and even though he lost weight it
took them twenty minutes to carry him down the spiral
staircase in a big orange tarp IT WAS NOT PRETTY.
Put Mom on.

(**MOM** *appears, wearing a housecoat and an old-fash-
ioned nurse's cap.*)

Mom hello you sound so tired how are you…Mom says
this and this and this and then she says

MOM. Are you sure you want to come home?

(*She disappears.*)

ANIMA. After the phone went down again I told naked Him
that she had asked me that. She's not thinking right
now, he said, with all the authority of a piece of wet
seaweed.
I called her back and you know what I was thinking?
Boy, when I get phone bill next month I'm going to
see this date and this call and remember it was the day
I lost my male parent. I also thought about meeting
new people years from now and telling them about this
and them asking me

PEOPLE. *(offstage)* Are you okay?

ANIMA. And me tucking a flyaway hair behind my ear and saying, "I'm okay now. It was difficult at first. But I'm okay now."

SO. I made phone calls up the wazoo while Mr. Helpful Caring Seaweed – sorry, he was wonderful and I am evil but I'm relatively okay with that – made a list of stuff for me and people to contact while I was gone oh fuck I have to get a plane ticket from LAX to Jersey but it will be nice to be on the east coast again because GOD I HATE IT OUT HERE no one wears black and it is always sunny and the smog gives me acne worse than a prepubescent boy working the grill at Roy Rogers and they don't even have Roy Rogers out here only Arby's can you believe that and I don't own a car and I miss the city and I miss the bars that don't close at one in the morning on a Saturday night and the rain and people who look fat and ugly in bathing suits and our creepy little Jersey-ghetto apartment with the moldy bathroom tiles and my father.

Called the airlines and got stuck in a pot hole until I screamed BEREAVEMENT RATE or something equally dramatic and they hopped to it like I was bathed in sepia tones shooting at their heels yelling dance dagnamit dance

Then.

I danced and He danced until my bag was packed buh-bye I'll miss you little apartment too bad I don't have plants or I'd tell you to water them while I was gone so you could come into my empty apartment and fill it up a little at a time so it wouldn't be so empty when I came back. But I have no plants because plants and me aren't copacetic you see because I kill them and they DIE.

But even dead plants would be welcome as I said goodbye to the inorganic walls and the plasticmetalwood that I knew I would eventually return to, only much different then. Now was my last time to look upon my refrigerator and my coffee table and the wine bottle covered in dripped wax that my roomate and I had been so giddy over before she fled the coop and my computer that I had gotten such a good deal on and my closet space that is too big for one small person with no money, my last time to gaze upon this dome of wreckage before it became wreckage, the last time to see these objects in the BEFORE and not the AFTER, the fat and not the skinny,

which began

right now

(**ANIMA** *curls up onto the floor in her former position and resumes her wheezing.*)

(**CHRISTA** *enters with a tape player and a life-sized kneeling plastic statue of the Virgin Mary, complete with exposed bleeding heart.*)

(**CHRISTA** *presses play. James Taylor's "Sweet Baby James" begins to play.* **CHRISTA** starts to cry.*)

ANIMA. Who okay cramp what tongue floorwax ow forehead I need a drink.

CHRISTA. You have a bucket of dead flowers moldering in the corner

ANIMA. I don't own a vase

CHRISTA. Can I throw them out

ANIMA. No

(**ANIMA** *gestures to the statue.*)

What is that

CHRISTA. The Mexican family next door is having a yard sale, I think it's a lawn ornament, it was only three bucks

ANIMA. You a Jesus freak

CHRISTA. No, I just thought she would be nice company, bring some luck/

ANIMA. *(Mexican accent, overlapping)* Ave Maria, Nosotra Mujer

*See MUSIC USE note on page 3.

CHRISTA …at least she's vertical

ANIMA. *(slowly rising)* I'm getting there…I prefer the room bare

CHRISTA. It's a shame for you I'm paying half the rent

ANIMA. Just ace the music and we'll be fine…if it were up to me we'd have a great ceremonial burning of all the folk tapes in the western world and watch them melt into big stringy puddles of toxins while we all get high on the fumes

CHRISTA. I'll buy headphones

    (CHRISTA shuts her tape player off.)

ANIMA. Why are you crying

CHRISTA. Nothing, the brainiac bastards in my cohort were slicing me to bits on the steps of the history building

ANIMA. Why?

CHRISTA. I wasn't exactly luminous in seminar

ANIMA. Fuck 'em. Would you like a drink?

CHRISTA. No, thanks

    (ANIMA gets up to fix CHRISTA a drink.)

CHRISTA. She walks. Beginning to think you were stitched to the carpet

ANIMA. You figured if you stepped over me enough times I'd eventually/

CHRISTA. Should I have called an ambulance, what

ANIMA. No, it's what I needed, my lollipop roommate straddling my line of vision twice a day so I could check out her lacey underpants

CHRISTA. That's nasty

ANIMA. There was no where else to look, hell of a lot more interesting than the carpet

CHRISTA. I thought you were in the throes of some massive emotional calamity

ANIMA. I was. Your underpants got me through it

    (They both laugh. CHRISTA touches ANIMA's arm.)

CHRISTA. How are you though, really/

(**ANIMA** *jerks away angrily.*)

ANIMA. No

CHRISTA. *(frustrated)* Christ, I don't know how to act here

ANIMA. Don't act for starters, your compassion reeks like old garbage

CHRISTA. Okay, roommate, as long as I am living here with you I flat out refuse to tiptoe around you anymore or feel sorry for you or kiss your lumpy ass unless you make an effort to wipe the drool off your chin once in a while

ANIMA. That. That's how I want it between us. No bullshit.

(**ANIMA** *hands* **CHRISTA** *her drink.*)

CHRISTA. What is this?

ANIMA. Jack Daniels

CHRISTA. Aren't you supposed to put something in it

ANIMA. What, like a straw

CHRISTA. No, like Pepsi or something

ANIMA. Um, no.

CHRISTA. Well. To no bullshit.

(*They clink and drink.* **CHRISTA** *gags.*)

ANIMA. You get used to it.

(**ANIMA** *lights a cigarette.*)

Last week I bit my tongue in my sleep and warm blood filled my mouth and I woke up choking on it so I ran into the bathroom and spit into the sink and watched my mouth-blood drip down the drain and I kept thinking, somewhere beneath the dirty streets of Los Angeles my blood was mingling with the blood of bitten tongues and bloody gums and children's elbows and addicts' noses and teenage girls' underpants, and for the first time in weeks I wasn't lonely.

You. Make it bloody.

(*a beat*)

CHRISTA. Six years ago my sister and her adonis boyfriend and I were at a county fair and she wanted to go up in the ferris wheel but no one else did so she went up by herself and after a minute the gears stuck and adonis was standing next to me laughing through his nose making snort sounds and in a blinding moment I saw he didn't love her and then he had me behind the slurpie hut with my flower print dress hiked up around my waist and my hair wrapped around his knuckles. I bled a little.

ANIMA. Cocksucker.

CHRISTA. I asked him to.

ANIMA. Oh.

(a beat)

CHRISTA. I never told anyone that before. Sounds so strange out loud.

ANIMA. Better out loud then forever echoing in the caverns of your unrequited guilt

(ANIMA smiles. CHRISTA drinks.)

(Lights up on CHRISTA in seminar.)

CHRISTA. And so, this text can most persuasively be read as an imaginative reconciliation of historically-contingent tensions in social identification, thus awarding us insights into a bohemian woman's complex and under-analyzed notions of selfhood.

(She looks up. Silence.)

Um, and ultimately I, um, plan to show how such females imaginatively reworked the definition of une femme bourgeoise, selectively patching together deeply embedded, um, Republican ideals of work, marriage, and, um, intellectual cultivation.

(silence)

That's all.

(Lights up on JENNA, KELLEE and DAVIE smoking Marlboros with their heads tilted at very condescending angles. They are wearing one large outfit that connects them all.)

DAVIE, JENNA KELLE. Tripe. Utter tripe. A waste of my fucking imagination..

JENNA. Her thematic premise was

KELLEE, DAVIE. Unsupported

JENNA. Her argument was

KELLEE, DAVIE. Sprawling

JENNA. Her research reeked of flabuosity

DAVIE, KELLE. Is this what the state schools are churning
  out these days

JENNA. Clearly.

DAVIE. Ga ga ga ga.

KELLEE, JENNA. And she was so

KELLEE. Apprehensive, mousy

DAVIE. I don't think she has the chops

KELLEE, JENNA. She's altogether

DAVIE. Chopless

  (They cackle. **CHRISTA** *enters, wearing a flower print
  skirt. They do not see her.)*

JENNA. How in the world is she fully funded?

KELLEE. She's fully funded?

DAVIE. She's got the Klemer grant AND the Walker AND a
  TA-ship.

JENNA. So arbitrary! Fa-da ga ga

DAVIE, JENNA. Fa-da ga ga!

KELLEE. And her skirt

JENNA, DAVIE. No

KELLEE. Elastic waist

JENNA, DAVIE. No

KELLEE. Flowerprint

JENNA, DAVIE. Ross Dress For Less

  (They cackle. **DAVIE** *spots* **CHRISTA.***)*

DAVIE. Christa…

CHRISTA. Hi.

JENNA. Hi.

KELLEE. Hi.

CHRISTA. Hi.

KELLEE, JENNA, DAVIE. Congrats on your presentation today.

DAVIE. Tough break, being first and all

KELLEE. Ambitious topic

JENNA. You seemed rather....

DAVIE. How do you think it went

KELLEE. Ga ga?

CHRISTA. It's hard to say...I'm late for a meeting...see you...

(She exits.)

DAVIE. Bye.

JENNA. Bye.

KELLEE. Bye.

(a beat)

DAVIE. Snooty-patooty.

(Back in **ANIMA** *and* **CHRISTA***'s apartment.* **CHRISTA** *is sitting on the couch studying.* **ANIMA** *has her books on the floor, trying to study, eating chips loudly. She can't concentrate. She walks over to the bar and makes two drinks. She hands one to* **CHRISTA***.)*

CHRISTA. It's only five o'clock

ANIMA. Not in Fiji...everything is relative

CHRISTA. Do you do this every day?

ANIMA. Yes.

CHRISTA. I don't know if I can keep up.

ANIMA. Your job isn't to keep up. Your job is to be infinitely fascinating to me...

*(***ANIMA** *leans over and checks out* **CHRISTA***'s work.)*

So what do you study?

CHRISTA. It's boring history stuff

ANIMA. Then bore me.

CHRISTA. I study the conflict of women in bohemian circles at the turn of the century in France

ANIMA. What was their conflict

CHRISTA. They were caught between the need to remain reserved and orderly versus their desire to tear through the streets and engage in lascivious practices

ANIMA. Oooh, what, like pagan rituals, virgin sacrifices

CHRISTA. No, no. Sex. Booze. Café life, theatre houses, music halls.

ANIMA. Jeepers. I kinda pictured them all dainty, spinning parasols and nibbling baguettes

CHRISTA. *(giddy)* They were a little wild. They dressed in men's clothing, they smoked opium, they had many many lovers of both sexes...YET. They saved money scrupulously. They made and mended their own clothes. They kept records of their expenses. They retained every last one of their domestic sensibilities.

ANIMA. Why?

CHRISTA. Their education required it.

ANIMA. That's pretty lame.

CHRISTA. THAT is a new model of the bourgeois female.

*(**ANIMA** raises her glass.)*

ANIMA. La Vie Boheme....

*(**ANIMA** drinks.)*

CHRISTA. Am I getting insipid yet?

ANIMA. Don't worry, you'll have plenty of warning. My eyes will start to roll in concentric circles.

CHRISTA. What should I do?

ANIMA. Hose me down. Feed me pastries. Send for back-up.

CHRISTA. Got it.

(They giggle and drink.)
*(Lights up on **CHRISTA** filming her room.)*

CHRISTA. As you can see, Camera, my room is nearly complete. Books arranged by genre, clothing in ascending quality order, tapes and CD's filed by temporal mood sequence. Even got my posters up. I suggested to The Roommate we put that one in the living room, but she started howling, "I HATE Anne Geddes, who the fuck thinks sticking a kid in cabbage is cute?" I thought everyone did.

But we talked again today. We're talking. She intrigues me. I like her. I like her, Camera.

(Lights up on the apartment. A tidy tower of video tapes is stacked in the corner where the dead flowers used to be, along side the empty bucket.)

(ANIMA passes CHRISTA a joint and lights it for her.)

ANIMA. If your cohort could see you now

CHRISTA. They'd roast me alive over their glowing cigarette butts

ANIMA. Ah, they're all a bunch of puffed up ass-lickers

CHRISTA. I want them to like me

ANIMA. You want them to respect you

CHRISTA. That too. But their minds think differently than mine, more analytically and globally and philosophically

ANIMA. That's training, not intellect

CHRISTA. You don't understand

ANIMA. I'm in grad school too

CHRISTA. It's different

ANIMA. How so

CHRISTA. You study theatre.

ANIMA. Um, fuck you?

CHRISTA. Your masters is terminal, you don't get all the academic posing that goes with a PhD.

ANIMA. Right.

CHRISTA. I don't know how to act around them. I know my field, it's not like I'm incompetent, why can't I just…I lack…..

ANIMA. My flowers

CHRISTA. What

ANIMA. In the bucket, where'd you put them

CHRISTA. I threw them out

ANIMA. When

CHRISTA. This morning, I was cleaning, what

ANIMA. You just threw them out, I asked you not to/

CHRISTA. There was grey fuzz growing on the stems, they stank up the corner, sweetie, we'll buy more tomorrow

ANIMA. I don't fucking want more

CHRISTA. Then we'll get something else, a plant, something that won't die when you stick it in a bucket

(a beat)

I'm sorry/

ANIMA. Fine. Whatever. They were dead.

CHRISTA. I didn't realize/

ANIMA. Forget it.

(a beat)

CHRISTA. You want to read my paper?

ANIMA. Now?

CHRISTA. Yes…No…Whenever…

ANIMA. I may not understand everything…

CHRISTA. I think you will. I'll print it out for you. Later.

ANIMA. Okay.

CHRISTA. Good. 'Cause it's hot shit.

(**CHRISTA** *takes another hit. There is a knock on the door.*)

ANIMA. Who the fuck is it

(**CHRISTA** *stands and peeks out the peephole.*)

CHRISTA. Some skinny erudite-looking fellow

(**ANIMA** *stands and looks through the peephole.*)

ANIMA. Excuse me…

(ANIMA runs out of the room.)

CHRISTA. Ann…

*(Another knock. **CHRISTA** opens the door. It's **ALAN**.)*

ALAN. Hi…does Annie still live here?

CHRISTA. Yes, I think she's in the bathroom. I'm Christa.

ALAN. Alan, friend from school. I live around the corner.

CHRISTA. I just moved in. First year grad student.

ALAN. Theatre?

CHRISTA. History.

ALAN. I studied history in undergrad.

CHRISTA. Really?

ALAN. What's your field?

CHRISTA. French intellectual history. Belle époque

ALAN. Ah, the fin de siécle

CHRISTA. Why do you say it like that

ALAN. The last gasp of a decadent society confident in its own inevitable progress

CHRISTA. But the greatest challenge to the Enlightenment's notion of reasonable man, n'est pas?

ALAN. Oui, c'est vrai…

(a beat)

I just came to return some CD's

(He hands her a bag.)

There are a few T-shirts in there too

CHRISTA. Don't you want to come in?

*(**ALAN** glances in the direction of the bathroom.)*

ALAN. I think maybe no. I've got a ton of work. Please tell her I stopped by and I hope she's feeling better.

CHRISTA. No problem.

ALAN. Maybe I'll see you on campus.

CHRISTA. Nice meeting you

*(**ALAN** exits. **ANIMA** enters.)*

CHRISTA. Why did you run off?

ANIMA. Is he gone?

CHRISTA. Yes. He was cute.

ANIMA. What did he want?

CHRISTA. He hopes you're feeling better and brought you these

> (**CHRISTA** *hands* **ANIMA** *the bag.* **ANIMA** *looks inside.*)

ANIMA. Wow. That, that hurts

> (*She kneels on the floor.*)

CHRISTA. Ann…

ANIMA. In a bag

CHRISTA. Who is he, an ex, what…

> (**ANIMA** *curls up on the floor, wheezing.*)

Come on, sweetie, let's talk about it, talk to me…

> (*She does not.* **CHRISTA** *sits on the floor next to* **ANIMA** *and strokes her back.*)

> (**ALAN** *returns and begins circling* **ANIMA.** **CHRISTA** *does not see him.*)

ALAN. I am thirty-two, nine years older than you. I have penetrated nineteen women, not including you, with my average sized penis. I played the viola all through college and a bit professionally before graduate school, I floss my teeth to NPR twice a day, each night I use lotion from a little blue jar to keep me from getting wrinkly, I have an austere set of political beliefs, I am a vegan, I read the Los Angeles Times spread across my carpet every morning, I shop at Trader Joe's for all my groceries and I use only raw unprocessed honey in my tea.

You eat rare meat, you listen to top forty radio, you never read the paper, you drink Bud Ice and you've only slept with two men, one of whom was gay. What on God's good earth ever made you think it would work between us?

> (*He disappears.* **ANIMA** *crawls into* **CHRISTA**'*s lap.*)

(**CHRISTA** *rocks* **ANIMA** *gently and begins singing James Taylor's "Smiling Face."* A beat.*)

ANIMA. Is that James Taylor

CHRISTA. What happens if it is

ANIMA. My brain explodes in your lap

CHRISTA. Oh. Then no.

ANIMA. Good.

(**CHRISTA** *continues to rock* **ANIMA** *and sing. The statue of Mary behind* **CHRISTA** *and* **ANIMA** *begins to sway to the music.* **ANIMA** *notices and says nothing.*)

(*Lights up on the apartment. The video tapes are now in a tape holder. The empty bucket is still in the corner of the room.*)

(**CHRISTA** *runs through the room, clutching several bags, and exits into the bedroom.*)

(*A moment later,* **ANIMA** *stumbles with* **SUSAN**, *a slightly hysterical houseplant. She struggles with it, dragging it into the center of the room.*)

ANIMA. Don't worry…I got it…no need for/

CHRISTA. *(offstage)* I'm changing/

ANIMA. You couldn't wait until we got it out of it from the car?

CHRISTA. *(offstage)* I have to know. The mirrors were slimming, the lights were tinted pink/

(**ANIMA** *steps back and squints at the plant.*)

ANIMA. Maybe we should have measured before we bought this.

CHRISTA. *(offstage)* Too big?

ANIMA. It's sort of digesting everything in the room.

CHRISTA. *(offstage)* Maybe we could keep it on the terrace.

ANIMA. I think I kinda love it.

CHRISTA. *(offstage)* I can't believe I spent so much money. I don't have any money. What the hell makes me think I can afford a new wardrobe? I never do this. I'm losing my mind/

*See MUSIC USE note on page 3

ANIMA. Shut yer hole.

(**CHRISTA** *enters, wearing a gorgeous, completely flattering, stylish dress.*)

CHRISTA. Ahem.

(**ANIMA** *turns and gapes.*)

ANIMA. Shit on a stick, Chris…

CHRISTA. It's not too much, is it…it's only a daytime thing, but everyone else will be dressed up…

ANIMA. You're disarming

CHRISTA. Never been called that before

ANIMA. I mean really. You are one hot bitch. Your cohorts are gonna gag on their expensive vocabularies

CHRISTA. Thank you for picking it out. I wouldn't have looked twice at it by myself.

ANIMA. Sure you would've

CHRISTA. It's not really me…

ANIMA. How do you feel in it?

CHRISTA. Like one of those frilly edible sugar holiday ornaments they stick on cakes

ANIMA. Is that good or bad.

CHRISTA. I can't tell. I think good.

(**ANIMA** *picks up the camcorder and films* **CHRISTA** *as she poses and twirls.*)

CHRISTA. Will you do my hair tomorrow

ANIMA. How do you want it

CHRISTA. Sorta classy sorta trashy

ANIMA. My specialty. Go pose with the newest member of the household

(**CHRISTA** *approaches the plant.*)

CHRISTA. Hm

ANIMA. You hate it.

CHRISTA. It's got stage presence…

ANIMA. You liked it in the store

CHRISTA. Next to the other plants it waxed exotic…here it's borderline macabre

ANIMA. But it's the first product of our sanctified union as roommates

CHRISTA. Our lovechild

ANIMA. Yes

CHRISTA. He or she

ANIMA. Come now

CHRISTA. What shall we call her

ANIMA. Something joyful, non-pretentious yet entirely unique

CHRISTA. Susan.

*(**ANIMA** aims the camcorder at the plant.)*

ANIMA. Our baby Susan.

*(**CHRISTA** slips her arm around **ANIMA**'s waist. They regard the plant a moment.)*

CHRISTA. My pits are sweating.

ANIMA. Doofus, go change

*(**CHRISTA** runs off.)*

*(**ANIMA** begins to drag the plant toward the corner of the room and notices the empty bucket. She stares at it quietly a moment. Lights change. It is the past.)*

*(**ALAN** enters and hands a large bouquet of wildflowers to **ANIMA**.)*

ALAN. How you doing, kiddo

ANIMA. Super actually, I'm flabbergasting myself. Thanks

(She takes the flowers and looks around for somewhere to put them. She grabs the bucket from the corner of the room.)

ANIMA. You won't be offended if I stick 'em in here

ALAN. You don't own a vase

ANIMA. I don't own anything. There's some rainwater left, how's that for recycling

(She sticks the flowers in the bucket and puts it back in the corner of the room.)

ALAN. When did you get back from Jersey

ANIMA. Just now. Listen, thank you for everything/

ALAN. Don't thank/

ANIMA. And I'm sorry I was so mean to you before I left, I was a little overwhelmed. Hug me now

*(They hug. **ALAN** pulls away.)*

ALAN. You smell like liquor.

ANIMA. It's a long flight and the bottles are so cute, I saved you one, so what did you do while I was away

ALAN. Hung out with friends

ANIMA. Anyone I know?

ALAN. No, they were friends from college

ANIMA. You and your 'friends from college', you decorate yourself with a billion people each night, dangle them from your ears and wrists as you spin though the city and you never think to ask me along

ALAN. You weren't here

ANIMA. Before, dildo

ALAN. You get drunk too fast, you're like a seven car pile up at the bottom of an icy hill

ANIMA. Aw you pussy, it's fun

ALAN. Sometimes

ANIMA. You had fun that night in O'Brien's with me and then at Denny's later, we were both ripped out of our gourds

ALAN. You licked your salad plate

ANIMA. What?

ALAN. At Denny's. You finished all the lettuce and tomatoes and you placed the plate to your face and licked it in a circle

ANIMA. I did not. There was more dressing left.

(a beat)

Aren't you going to ask me how it went at home

ALAN. I'm afraid to

ANIMA. Don't worry it was all very appropriate, grand-mother sang a little tune called "How I wish God would Take me too" and danced a jig before all the dearly-beerlies, and oh man the cold cut platters fruit baskets condolence cards…and of course, Jesus at every turn. He's with Jesus now. We should thank Jesus he felt little pain. Would you like some Jesus with your dinner ma'am

But what really snapped my strap was when the priest handed Artie the flag. No one knew he was going to do that. He whipped it off the casket and folded it up into a neat triangle like a cut sandwich and said "On behalf of the President of the United States I present this flag to you in honor of your father's service…" It was wild. I felt for a second my dad WAS the president. Assassinated. By his fellow countrymen. Bastard capi-talist corporate American dream, live it love it fuck it in the ass or it will fuck you ha ha ha – you think I'm crazy, don't you/

ALAN. No sweetie, you're overwrought and drunk

ANIMA. I'm not overwrought. I'm just plain wrought, like iron…so who missed me

ALAN. Everyone asked about you

ANIMA. Who

ALAN. The department, anyone who knows you

ANIMA. Why do you think they supposed *you* knew?

ALAN. I sent out a memo that we've been sleeping together

ANIMA. Shut up

ALAN. We agreed, kiddo/

ANIMA. I know, I was there, I just don't remember anymore

ALAN. Don't pretend/

ANIMA. Because it could get weird. Well it's already weird. I can't look across the room at you in Seminar without thinking I know how that man tastes, and then when you quote Chekhov or Brecht with a flip of your thin wrist I could just come right there in my good skirt all that inspiration dripping down my legs…then not be allowed to touch you, to even glance steamily in your direction…

I mean don't you think they can sense the buzzing air between us

ALAN. They don't know/

ANIMA. Let's fuck

ALAN. No

ANIMA. Come on, I read somewhere it's perfectly natural for someone who has just experienced great loss to have an elevated libido

ALAN. Where

ANIMA. Reader's fucking Digest.

ALAN. No Annie

ANIMA. It's been a while, it won't take me long

ALAN. I have to go/

ANIMA. Please Alan

ALAN. I'll call you tomorrow

ANIMA. I don't want to be alone

ALAN. My plants need watering/

ANIMA. Alan.

(**ALAN** *does not answer.*)

What. What. Just fucking say it.

(*a beat*)

ALAN. I didn't want to bring this up so soon after your/
ANIMA. (*overlapping*) Ah. Yes.

ALAN. tragedy and all I didn't handle this the best way/
ANIMA. (*overlapping*) Handle. Great

(*a beat*)

ALAN. I can't do this, Annie. There's not enough of me.
ANIMA. Do

ALAN. This. Any of it. I'm sorry.

(*a beat*)

ANIMA. It's okay. Well, it's not, really. Goodbye.

> (**ALAN** *leaves.* **ANIMA** *drops to her knees. Lights change to normal. The flowers are gone from the bucket.*)

CHRISTA. *(offstage)* Annie?

ANIMA. Yeah

CHRISTA. *(offstage)* You alright?

ANIMA. Yeah, why

CHRISTA. *(offstage)* Dunno…thought I heard you wheezing

> (**ANIMA** *stands and pushes the plant into the corner.*)

> (**CHRISTA** *emerges and notices the plant's new position.*)

CHRISTA. Ooh, much better.

> (**CHRISTA** *slips her arm around* **ANIMA***'s waist again. They regard the plant a moment.*)

CHRISTA. Oh my God, I really do feel like a parent

ANIMA. Yeah

CHRISTA. I care what happens to her all of a sudden

ANIMA. Me too

CHRISTA. I want to buy her the best plant food and send her to the best plant schools

ANIMA. Yeah

CHRISTA. And on Sunday mornings we'll get in savage arguments about her boyfriends

ANIMA. Ha

CHRISTA. And someday she'll marry and have little sprouts of her own

> *(a beat)*

Are you gonna tell me what's wrong

ANIMA. Nothing

CHRISTA. Did I do something? Are you mad at me?

ANIMA. *(vicious)* Not everything is about you, Christa.

> *(a beat)*

CHRISTA. *(taken aback)* I never said it was/

ANIMA. I need some air

(**ANIMA** *exits.* **CHRISTA** *stares after her, then at the plant.*)

(*Lights up on the dinner table.* **MOM** *and* **ARTIE** *are seated around empty platters, cutting imaginary food.*)

(**ARTIE** *is wearing a huge diaper and* **MOM** *wears her nurse's hat. There are two empty chairs, each with a place setting.*)

(**ANIMA** *appears and takes her seat at the table.*)

MOM. It's a shame your sister can't be here I cooked her favorite tonight

ARTIE. Yeah

ANIMA. I'm right here, Ma/

MOM. It's shrimp scampi, I never used to cook it because Daddy hated it but since Daddy died I can make it every night

ARTIE. Yeah

ANIMA. Mom, there's nothing on the plates/

MOM. You like your shrimp scampi Artie

ARTIE. Yeah

MOM. Your sister loved it, she had a face like milk and eyes like wet September but Oh how Daddy would hit her I remember one time she dropped a bowl of chicken soup on the floor when she was twenty and he beat her to the ground, you remember that Artie?

ARTIE. Yeah

MOM. The dog was barking and Gramma was screaming and Daddy was flailing away and your sister was just sitting there on the kitchen floor in a puddle of soup and blood and she wasn't crying, you remember that, Artie.

ARTIE. Yeah

MOM. And what was that cute thing you were shouting

ARTIE. Call the cops

MOM. Call the cops, that's right, what fun, we haven't had fun like that since Daddy died, have we Artie

ARTIE. No

MOM. No we sure haven't. I wish your sister was here, she loves to reminisce. Doesn't she, Artie?

ARTIE. Yeah.

MOM. Yes, she does, she sure does

(Lights up on **CHRISTA** *studying.* **ANIMA** *enters holding a half-empty bottle of Jack Daniels.)*

ANIMA. I want to tell you something.

CHRISTA. I know.

ANIMA. I want to but I don't know how.

CHRISTA. Try saying it slowly

ANIMA. Okay.

(a beat)

He.

CHRISTA. Who.

ANIMA. Was losing his mind.

CHRISTA. Who

ANIMA. Just. Listen.

The last time I saw him alive was Christmas. I was reading in my room after our frozen turkey dinners and they were all watching The Nutcracker in the living room, I walked into the kitchen to get a glass of water and found him standing at the kitchen sink with his back to me. He was on his tiptoes pissing into the sink. I breathed out and he quickly came back down and zipped up, told me to get the hell out of there and into bed, and he walked out of the kitchen.

I stood there for twenty minutes not moving. It was seven-thirty at night. Everyone was still awake. My father was six-foot two and over two hundred pounds. The bathroom was closer to the living room than the kitchen.

How can I ever begin to find a way to talk about anything

CHRISTA. You just did.

*(A beat. **CHRISTA** strokes **ANIMA**'s hair. They sit in silence for a moment.)*

ANIMA. I have something for you. To help you out tomorrow

*(**ANIMA** holds out her empty palm.)*

CHRISTA. What is it

ANIMA. An Invisible Thingie. It's supposed to elevate your intellect and social dexterity.

CHRISTA. You're so thoughtful. What do I do with it

ANIMA. Eat it

CHRISTA. How, I can't even see it/

ANIMA. Eat it, quick, it's evaporating/

*(**CHRISTA** slams her face into **ANIMA**'s hands and pretends to eat something. They fall back in bed laughing hysterically.)*

CHRISTA. It better work

ANIMA. It will. I promise.

*(Lights up on **CHRISTA** in her dress with her hair styled. She is holding her camcorder at her side and chatting casually with someone.)*

CHRISTA ...I'm not arguing that, I'm saying the Third Republic's pedagogical initiative combined a glorification of hard work and a highly gendered system of values emphasizing public masculinity and private femininity with a call to cultivate one's vie interièure... oui, c'est tres interessant pour moi parçe-que j'adore cette epoch et l'idée de la femme bourgeoise nouvelle...oui...

*(**CHRISTA** touches her dress as if someone referred to it and laughs shyly.)*

Ma ensemble? Merci...merci beaucoup...

*(Lights up on **JENNA**, **KELLEE** and **DAVIE** smoking Marlboros with their heads tilted at very condescending angles, wearing the outfit.)*

DAVIE, JENNA. Girl was

KELLEE. On fire

DAVIE, JENNA. Her argument was

KELLEE. edgy, tongue-in-cheek with a healthy nod to

DAVIE, JENNA. Tradition

DAVIE. The paradoxical nature of

KELLEE, JENNA. Class identity

DAVIE. Modern conceptions of

KELLEE, JENNA. The self

DAVIE. Referencing shit left and right

KELLEE, JENNA. In French

DAVIE, KELLEE. Takes chops

> (**CHRISTA** *enters. They do not see her.*)

JENNA. And her hair was fabulicious

KELLEE. GA GA GA!

DAVIE. Takes chops

KELLEE. And her dress

DAVIE, JENNA. I could never get away with that

> (**DAVIE** *spots* **CHRISTA.**)

DAVIE. Christa…

CHRISTA. Hi.

JENNA. Hi.

KELLEE. Hi.

CHRISTA. Hi.

KELLEE. Super dress.

JENNA. Great hair.

DAVIE. Saw you chatting with Hudon today.

KELLEE. (*simultaneous*) Did he give you any feedback on your project?

JENNA. (*simultaneous*) Will he present at the Modern Historical Society?

DAVIE. (*simultaneous*) Is he mad and lecherous and rumpled and wise?

CHRISTA. I'm sorry, guys...I'm late for a meeting...see you...

(She exits smiling.)

DAVIE. Bye.

JENNA. Bye.

KELLEE. Bye.

(a beat)

DAVIE, JENNA, KELLEE. Chops.

(Lights up on **ANIMA.***)*

ANIMA. Hi Christa, it's Annie. I'm at fucking Mocha Joe's on Pico and I'm locked out of the apartment. Someone walked off with my bag. People suck. Hope your hair is holding up.

(Lights up on **CHRISTA** *seated at a library table, reading, still wearing the dress and the hairdo.)*

*(***ALAN** *enters carrying a bunch of books.)*

ALAN. Christa, right?

CHRISTA. Oh...you startled me

ALAN. I'm sorry...I'm/

CHRISTA. Alan. I remember. CD's and T-shirts.

ALAN. Right. I'm surprised you didn't catch me leering over there at you

CHRISTA. You were leering

ALAN. Well, not – I thought I knew you but couldn't remember how. You look different, all done up. That came out rather unfortunate. You looked fine before, but...why don't I just go leap into traffic.

CHRISTA. *(laughing)* Believe me, this is the first and last time you'll see me looking like this. My department had a big important luncheon today.

ALAN. Oooh. For what

CHRISTA. Schmooze-fest. I shmoozed. I NEVER shmooze.

*(***ALAN** *gestures to the camcorder.)*

ALAN. You filmed it?

CHRISTA. I film everything. Got all the major players on tape

ALAN. Doing what

CHRISTA. Masticating, proselytizing, assailing all the nubile young co-eds

ALAN. Blackmail

CHRISTA. Hardly

(a beat)

ALAN. Well. Sorry to bother you, I just wanted to make sure Annie got her stuff okay

CHRISTA. She did.

ALAN. I'd been waiting to give them to her in class but she hasn't been going.

CHRISTA. Really?

ALAN. Not since she got back from Jersey.

CHRISTA. That's so strange.

ALAN. Everyone's a little worried. I've tried calling her but she won't talk to me. I don't know if she told you…

CHRISTA. Told me

ALAN. We were sort-of involved for a month or so over the summer

CHRISTA. A month? I'd assumed longer

ALAN. No, but it ended clumsily and I am totally to blame and I thought maybe she was…she might be/

CHRISTA. She doesn't talk about you. She's dealing with other things.

ALAN. Of course. I just thought I might have exacerbated it.

CHRISTA. She's doing amazingly well. She's a strong girl.

ALAN. I never doubted it.

(a beat)

Anyhoo. It was nice seeing you again.

CHRISTA. You too.

ALAN. Bye.

CHRISTA. Bye.

> (**ALAN** *exits.* **CHRISTA** *returns to her reading.* **ALAN** *returns again.*)

ALAN. Sorry. I just…the graduate students association is having happy hour at O'Brien's tonight. Every department is invited. I think it's open bar. Don't know if you heard…

CHRISTA. I didn't

ALAN. It's a good opportunity for first-years to meet some people outside their department. Thought you might like to know. And please tell Annie.

CHRISTA. Thanks.

ALAN. No problem. Bye.

CHRISTA. Bye.

> (**ALAN** *exits.* **CHRISTA** *returns to her reading.* **ALAN** *returns again.*)

ALAN. Sorry. I thought because you're new to the area you might need directions…

CHRISTA. Okay

ALAN. You make a left out the main entrance and go straight down Hilgard until you get to Weyburn, make a quick right, and it's on the next corner opposite the Exxon. Annie definitely knows where it is.

CHRISTA. Got it.

ALAN. Okay. See you.

CHRISTA. Bye.

> (**ALAN** *exits.* **CHRISTA** *returns to her reading. After a moment she looks up and stares after* **ALAN**.)

> (**CHRISTA** *and* **ANIMA** *appear in separate lights.*)

CHRISTA. Annie, it's me. There's a big ho-down for all the grad students at O'Briens tonight. I'm thinking about stopping by. I'm at the library right now…I'll guess I'll call again before I leave. Oh, your Invisible Thingie worked. Hee.

ANIMA. Hey, me again. I'm still at fucking Mocha Joe's. Just checking to see if you're there yet...Call here when you get in.

CHRISTA. Hey. It's almost eight. I'm heading over to O'Briens. Hopefully I'll meet you there. Bye.

ANIMA. Where are you? I'm at Dell's Saloon across the street. I'll be here all night. Come over when you get this.

(Lights up on **CHRISTA** *at the bar, alone. She is drinking a Jack Daniels.)*

*(***ALAN** *approaches, drink in hand.)*

ALAN. Hey there

CHRISTA. Hey

ALAN. You all by yourself over here

CHRISTA. I don't really know anyone...I'm waiting for Annie

ALAN. She's coming?

CHRISTA. Yes.

ALAN. Mind if I join you while you wait

CHRISTA. Not at all

(He sits.)

ALAN. What are you drinking?

CHRISTA. Jack

ALAN. Plain?

CHRISTA. I don't like it mixed with anything.

ALAN. Just like your roommie

(a beat)

So. Tell me.

CHRISTA. Yes?

ALAN. Whatever you like.

CHRISTA. Um...

ALAN. Your schmoozefest.

CHRISTA. No...

ALAN. Go on.

CHRISTA. It really wasn't all that fascinating.

ALAN. That's fine, I'm easily fascinated

CHRISTA. Um...Well. I used my meager french as much as I could. I managed only to float topics about which I was entirely informed.

ALAN. Such as

CHRISTA. My dissertation. Bourgeois feminine identity in the Belle Epoque.

ALAN. Ah yes...

CHRISTA. God, why does everyone act like it's this eternally boring topic?

ALAN. I didn't mean to sound/

CHRISTA. I'm using an entirely non-traditional approach...

ALAN. Of course, I, I didn't, whoa....

   (a beat.)

   Look, this, I, I'm not...

CHRISTA. No. It's...fine. Sorry.

   (a beat)

ALAN. So.

CHRISTA. So.

   (A beat. They drink.)

   (Lights up on ANIMA in a bar. She is very drunk.)

ANIMA. What a piece of work is man, how noble in reason, how infinite in faculty, in form and move and inespresso ada-mahble...That's Shakespeare. I know more. I played Hamlet once in college. It was for a video project but I was good. No one could believe a chick Hamlet could be so goddamn good.

Why not? Men played women's roles for years and years and years, no one had a problem. I made people CRY. Because I could *hear* them, assface. Snif-snif from behind me, honking into a hanky in front of me, wet gurgling noises on my right...That's a fucked up feeling, you know? People who don't even know you, they believe so hard in your lie they make it their own.

ANIMA. *(cont.)* I'm not going to tell you my fucking name. I'm not here to get hit on. I'm just having a cocktail.

(She drinks.)

An actor, really? Quite a rarity in these parts. No, I don't act anymore. I study. Eighteenth century theatre. No, Shakespeare was earlier. No, Tennessee Williams was later. No, Galileo was an astronomer. It's okay, everyone gets them mixed up.

Get off me. My friend is picking me up. My roomate. My new roomate. She's brilliant. She's going to be a doctor soon. She analyzes women. Not a fucking shrink. She just does, then she makes history out of it.

(She drinks. A beat.)

No, but thanks. She'll be here any minute. Because I know. She takes care of me.

*(Lights down on **ANIMA** and up on **ALAN** and **CHRISTA**. **CHRISTA**'s hair is down and she's holding her shoes in one hand and the camcorder in the other. They are bent in half laughing.)*

CHRISTA. Oh God, it hurts...

*(**CHRISTA** begins filming **ALAN**.)*

ALAN. So I'm guessing that place was sort of a karaoke bar for the over-sixty crowd

CHRISTA. If that man with the gold tooth sang The Impossible Dream one more time/

ALAN. We were getting the filthiest looks from that man

CHRISTA. Because you kept making me recite that damn poem during his crescendo

ALAN. Do it again

CHRISTA. You've had enough

ALAN. Please, I won't ask again, I promise

CHRISTA. What am I, the whore of the French language

*(**ALAN** grabs the camcorder from **CHRISTA** and begins filming her.)*

*(**CHRISTA** laughs and begins to spin.)*

CHRISTA. *(cont., singing)*
> Ja l'ai vu de mes propres yeux un soir,
> Une étoile luxueuse et clair
> J'ai plus rein à désirer
> Ainsi, je dit, "Pourquoi faire?"

ALAN. You know that makes absolutely no sense

CHRISTA. What do you want, I wrote it in seventh grade

ALAN. What were you trying to say

CHRISTA. Basically, I found a bright star one night and I wanted to make a wish but then I realized I had nothing to wish for because I already had everything I wanted

ALAN. Happy childhood

CHRISTA. One of the few and the proud

ALAN. The warm chats over pot roast with mom and pop, the big piles of christmas presents...

CHRISTA. *(ginning widely)* And I am entirely well adjusted and I love my family dearly and I have no suburban guilt whatsoever. Ta-da.

ALAN. I am alarmingly attracted to you right now

CHRISTA. Oh.

> *(a beat)*

> Interesting.

ALAN. Yes.

> *(a beat)*

CHRISTA. I gotta get home. I reek of garlic mushrooms and Jack.

ALAN. *(hungrily)* You do.

CHRISTA. Stop that

ALAN. What

CHRISTA. That thing with your eyes, that hungry thing

ALAN. I'm sorry

CHRISTA. You're not, that's totally on purpose

ALAN. You're right

CHRISTA. We're drunk

ALAN. Then it doesn't count

CHRISTA. What doesn't

ALAN. Me kissing you

CHRISTA. Fuck. Fuck.

ALAN. I'm going to kiss you now

CHRISTA. You can't

ALAN. I know

CHRISTA. Please don't

ALAN. Okay

> (**ALAN** *and* **CHRISTA** *kiss. A beat.*)

CHRISTA. Are you okay to drive

ALAN. No. You

CHRISTA. No

ALAN. We can go for a walk. We'll walk it off

CHRISTA. Okay

> (*They kiss again and don't stop.* **CHRISTA** *drops her shoes.*)

> (*Sound of breaking glass. Lights up on the apartment.* **SUSAN** *has lost a leaf.*)

> (**ANIMA** *is kneeling on the floor. Her right hand is bloody.*)

ANIMA. I'll throw out the rest of my weed. I'll never masturbate in a public bathroom again. I'll wash my sheets more than once a year. I'll eat more fruit. Whatever you fucking want. Just don't...please...

> (*The kneeling figure of* **MARY-ANDROGYNE** *raises her head.*)

MARY-ANDROGYNE. Don't what?

ANIMA. Let her be dead.

MARY-ANDROGYNE. Who?

ANIMA. You know who

MARY-ANDROGYNE. I have no control over that. Who the fuck you think I am?

ANIMA. Madre de Dios

MARY-ANDROGYNE. No, I'm Androgyne, champion of all the little confused boy-girls like you

ANIMA. I'm not confused

MARY-ANDROGYNE. Then why is it when you have been known to enthusiastically engage in the sport of male humpery are you so miserably in love with your roommate

ANIMA. I'm just worried about her

MARY-ANDROGYNE. And you want to fuck her

ANIMA. Go away!

MARY-ANDROGYNE. Ah, the tone of a struck nerve. Listen. She's not like you. Some people are meant to suffer and some aren't. Don't you dare drag her through your solitary sludge. Give her the James Taylor, the balloons, the feathers, and keep your goddamn piss and bile to yourself. Or you'll kill her like you killed your Daddy

ANIMA. I didn't kill him/

MARY-ANDROGYNE. Running off to California for grad school, launching him into a panic about the money/

ANIMA. I never asked him for a dime

MARY-ANDROGYNE. And what made you think he wouldn't feel responsible for you just the same? You found that letter from the IRS, you knew how deep he was in it, and you still ran off

(**ANIMA** *begins to cry.*)

ANIMA. I didn't...I...

MARY-ANDROGYNE. Oh. Oh, I'm sorry. Baby, my poor sweet plum, my sewage pile, don't be sad, Daddy's in heaven with the angels and he's watching you through his solar powered telescope and he's weeping saline solution and snot into the ocean and contaminating it, make him stop pumpkin, all the bikini girls on the beaches will have green hair by tomorrow...

ANIMA. I can't...

(MARY-ANDROGYNE returns to her kneeling position.)

(CHRISTA enters. There are grass stains on her dress at the knees and on her ass.)

CHRISTA. Oh my God, what happened/

ANIMA. I got locked out, I smashed through my window with a rock and got cut on the glass/

(CHRISTA takes ANIMA's hand and examines it.)

CHRISTA. You didn't wash it

ANIMA. I'm pretty wasted

CHRISTA. Doesn't look like you have any glass in there

ANIMA. It's just a cut

(CHRISTA runs into the kitchen and returns with a wet paper towel. She begins dabbing at ANIMA's wound.)

CHRISTA. What am I gonna do with you

ANIMA. You'll think of something

CHRISTA. We'll call the landlady tomorrow, tell her one of the kids across the street did it

ANIMA. Okay.

(a beat)

Your dress...

CHRISTA. Oh...I fell

ANIMA. Before or after the luncheon

CHRISTA. After

ANIMA. Thank God...how did it go?

CHRISTA. Your hair was a big hit

ANIMA. And the dress

CHRISTA. The dress

ANIMA. Belle of the ball, huh

CHRISTA. Girl

ANIMA. I told you I told you

CHRISTA. You did

ANIMA. Where'd you go after

CHRISTA. O'Brien's, I called to invite you...

ANIMA. Are you drunk too?

CHRISTA. Yeah

ANIMA. Wheee

>   *(They giggle and roll on the floor a bit.* **ANIMA** *grabs the camcorder and films* **CHRISTA.***)*

ANIMA. It's approximately three thirty on a Friday night and the roommates are drunk

CHRISTA. Don't, Annie

ANIMA. And tonight marks Mademoiselle Christa's grand ascent to the top of Mount Wonderful

CHRISTA. *(losing mirth)* Please

ANIMA. Will you let me do your hair when you're all famous and glittery

CHRISTA. Turn it off

ANIMA. What, your obsessive lust for documentation shuts down after midnight/

CHRISTA. OFF!

>   *(***ANIMA** *shuts off the camera. A beat.)*

ANIMA. Did you see Susan? She lost her first leaf.

CHRISTA. Should save it for the scrapbook

ANIMA. We have a scrapbook?

CHRISTA. We'll get one...

>   *(a beat)*

ANIMA ...sleepy

CHRISTA. Me too

ANIMA. Can't sleep in my room

CHRISTA. How come?

ANIMA. Someone broke the window

CHRISTA. Oh. You sleeping out here

ANIMA. Yeah...You wanna

CHRISTA. Want me to

ANIMA. Yeah

CHRISTA. 'Kay

    (**ANIMA** *lays down with her arm around* **CHRISTA.**)

ANIMA. Glad you're home

    (**ANIMA** *closes her eyes.* **CHRISTA** *does not.*)

    (**MARY-ANDROGYNE** *lifts her head to look at the sleeping couple.*)

End of Movement One

MOVEMENT TWO

(Lights up on **ANIMA**. **CHRISTA** *is gone.* **SUSAN** *has lost another leaf during the night.)*

(After a moment, **MARY-ANDROGYNE** *raises her head. She holds her stomach and screams as if she's giving birth. She then lifts her huge veil and from between her legs emerges* **ANGEL ONE** *with a guitar and* **ANGEL TWO** *with a harp [which she doesn't know how to play]. They wear leather fetish clothing.)*

*(***ANGEL ONE** *and* **ANGEL TWO** *gather around* **ANIMA** *and sing the following song in harmony as* **ANIMA** *wakes.)*

MARY-ANDROGYNE, ANGEL ONE & ANGEL TWO.
> She's in you now, now, oh now
> She's driving her little red civic through your veins
> And parking it by the bloodclot in your brain
> You would sing a sky of purple night for her
> For a coin tumbled from the corner of her eye
> You would drink the milk of a thousand running wounds, oh my
> And the battle field is ripe with them now
> And the children cry and cry
> Because they've lost their tongues

*(***ANIMA** *realizes* **CHRISTA** *is gone.)*

MARY-ANDROGYNE. She's gone. You put the moves on her

ANIMA. WHAT?

MARY-ANDROGYNE. Too drunk to remember? In the middle of the night you slid your hand beneath her shirt and cupped her left breast in your palm. You held it there for a little while, until she woke. Then you placed your

lips to her ear and quietly confessed everything. How
you stand outside the bathroom after she's showered
to bask in the lingering aroma of her clean hair. How
you get off to the image of her rubbing herself on your
knee/

ANIMA. No…

(The angels giggle.)

MARY-ANDROGYNE. She's off looking for a single apartment
right now. She'll finish packing when she returns.

*(**ANIMA** jumps up and runs into **CHRISTA**'s bedroom.
The angels giggle.)*

*(**ANIMA** emerges, angered.)*

ANIMA. Her things are still there

MARY-ANDROGYNE. So gullible

ANIMA. What the hell kind of deity are you?

MARY-ANDROGYNE. A dark one. I changed when you did

ANIMA. I haven't changed

MARY-ANDROGYNE. Mais oui, you have. Vous avez une mala-
die noire et grande/

ANIMA. Why are you speaking French?

MARY-ANDROGYNE. You tell me.

*(**CHRISTA** enters with pastry box.)*

ANIMA. Where'd you go?

CHRISTA. Hang-over pastries.

ANIMA. You are a superhero.

*(**ANIMA** digs into the box.)*

CHRISTA. It's so warm outside, I can't believe it's Octo-
ber, did you ever notice how all the palm trees bend
toward the ocean, I was trying to figure out if they
were stretching to get closer to the water or farther
away from the mountains

ANIMA. No idea, did you get any Boston Creams?

CHRISTA. They were out.

ANIMA. Those motherfuckers. How's your head?

CHRISTA. Fine. How's your hand

ANIMA. Fine

CHRISTA. Let me see.

> (CHRISTA *examines* ANIMA*'s hand as* ANIMA *eats a donut.*)

Have you been picking at it

ANIMA. Yes

CHRISTA. Stop. It needs to scab.

ANIMA. I can't help it

> (CHRISTA *disappears into the bathroom.*)

ANIMA. Susan lost another leaf...

> (CHRISTA *emerges with a bandaid and antiseptic, having not heard* ANIMA. *She begins cleaning* ANIMA*'s wound.*)

ANIMA. I read your paper yesterday.

CHRISTA. You did?

ANIMA. The whole thing.

CHRISTA. What did you think?

ANIMA. I loved it. I mean, my background in french history is not exactly comprehensive...but I was totally with it.

CHRISTA. Really?

ANIMA. Yeah. Like when Colette showed her tits on stage and they called her courageous. She's all bad-ass and brazen, like a DIVA. And it was pretty freaky to be inside your head like that. Freaky, freaky stuff.

CHRISTA. I'm so glad you liked it...

ANIMA. But it completely makes sense. Why you're interested in those women.

> (*a beat*)

CHRISTA. What do you mean?

ANIMA. You know. Neat, educated, middle-class. By-the-book all the way. Dying to get the fuck out and do a little hardcore shake-and-bake. But sorta...you know.

> (*a beat*)

Anyway. Good reading.

(a beat)

CHRISTA. How are the donuts.

ANIMA. Yummy.

CHRISTA. And how are classes?

ANIMA. Also yummy.

(**CHRISTA** *looks up at* **ANIMA.**)

What?

CHRISTA. You haven't been going.

ANIMA. Who told you

CHRISTA. A friend of yours.

ANIMA. WHO.

CHRISTA. A friend who was at the bar last night.

ANIMA. I have no friends.

CHRISTA. A classmate

ANIMA. Who who who?

CHRISTA. Tell me why you haven't been going to class first.

ANIMA. I haven't felt like it.

CHRISTA. Why not?

ANIMA. School makes me grouchy.

CHRISTA. Why don't you take a semester or two off?

ANIMA. For what? To remember why I'm supposed to be sad? I don't have to remember. It's my skin now.

CHRISTA. You can't just not go

ANIMA. One of my professors is this hundred-and-eighty-year-old Marxist evangelist who speaks extemporaneously for hours and makes grown men and women weep in class. Tears, I shit you not. But I never do. I try to look all enthralled but at the break I bolt from the room and burrow in the stairwell and scream into my sleeve.

CHRISTA. Maybe grad school isn't for you

ANIMA. What else is there?

CHRISTA. You tell me

ANIMA. If I knew that I wouldn't be here

CHRISTA. What do you like to do?

ANIMA. What do I like to do…I like to act. I'm a really good
actor. I did a lot of plays in college. Never got leads but
I always kicked ass in the bit parts. And I fucking love
theatre. The body fluids and cigarette smoke and bad
breath, the fucking, the drinking, the injured souls. I
want to do nasty plays. The kind where you get nekid
on stage and everyone stares at your nipples.

CHRISTA. You're clearly not an academic.

ANIMA. Yeah, but it's free. I'm playing ball with my finan-
cial hardship here. Now who's my friend.

CHRISTA. It was Alan. He's worried about you.

*(**ANIMA** is dead quiet. She pulls her bandaged hand
from **CHRISTA**'s grasp.)*

ANIMA. What else did he say?

CHRISTA. You haven't been returning his calls

ANIMA. What else

CHRISTA. I don't know

*(**ANIMA** grabs **CHRISTA**'s wrist.)*

ANIMA. He told you things

CHRISTA. You're hurting me

*(**ANIMA** lets go of **CHRISTA**'s wrist.)*

ANIMA. Don't. Listen to me. DO NOT take his side on this.

CHRISTA. Side, what are you talking about, you were only
seeing each other a month

*(**ANIMA** is quiet.)*

He's your friend and he cares about you/

ANIMA. I don't want to talk about it.

(a beat)

CHRISTA. Fine.

*(A beat. **ANIMA** walks over to the tapes. She begins playing with them.)*

What's on these?

CHRISTA. My entire life since freshman year when I got my camcorder

ANIMA. What are you saving them for

CHRISTA. Nothing. Myself. Someday I'll make an epic montage of all my favorite moments and set it to James Taylor's "Smiling Face."

ANIMA. You are a supreme freak.

CHRISTA. I know.

ANIMA. Let's watch 'em…

CHRISTA. I can't, I've got a meeting

ANIMA. On a Saturday

CHRISTA. With my cohort

ANIMA. Oh. Okay. I'll just watch 'em while you're gone.

CHRISTA. You wouldn't

ANIMA. What difference does it make, I don't know anybody in them

CHRISTA. Look, we'll watch them when I get home, okay?

ANIMA. Goodie. Are you naked in any of them?

CHRISTA. Only the ones with your mom

ANIMA. Score!

*(**CHRISTA** grabs her camcorder and her things to leave.)*

Is that one of the shirts we bought the other day?

CHRISTA. Yes.

ANIMA. I like it. Makes your boobs look all juicy. Like beefsteak tomatoes

CHRISTA. Thanks.

ANIMA. Don't be mad at me

CHRISTA. I'm not. I'm just late. I'll see you later.

*(She kisses **ANIMA** and exits.)*

*(After a moment **ANIMA** grabs a bag and begins stuffing **CHRISTA**'s video tapes into it. She prepares herself to exit.)*

*(On her way out the door she approaches **SUSAN** to inspect her leaves. She strokes them lovingly.)*

ANIMA. Tu es malade, ma petite plante. I will heal you

(**ANIMA** *tears off her bandage and drips some blood into* **SUSAN** *'s soil.*)

(*Lights up on* **ALAN**, *sitting, reading a book in a park.* **CHRISTA** *enters.* **ALAN** *stands.*)

ALAN. Hi

CHRISTA. Hi.

ALAN. How are you feeling

CHRISTA. Little fuzzy, you

ALAN. I'll be fine once the squirrels stop chewing so loud. You look beautiful.

CHRISTA. So do you.

(**ALAN** *kisses her tenderly.*)

ALAN. Pull up some grass, have a seat

CHRISTA. I think I need to stand.

(*a beat*)

ALAN. Uh-oh.

CHRISTA. I've been trying to find the most appropriate way to put this.

ALAN. I see.

(*a beat*)

Did you come up with something?

CHRISTA. Yes.

ALAN. Excellent.

(*a beat*)

Whenever you're ready.

CHRISTA. I had an amazing time with you last night.

ALAN. Glad to hear it.

CHRISTA. I mean a really amazing time. I haven't laughed that hard in months. And I never talk all night like that to someone I've just met.

ALAN. Neither do I.

CHRISTA. And afterwards, gosh

ALAN. It was.

CHRISTA. And I wanted to thank you for that, for all of it.

ALAN. You're welcome.

(a beat)

But.

CHRISTA. I think we should maybe consider/

ALAN. Never doing it again.

CHRISTA. I want, and I really mean this, for you and Annie to talk again.

ALAN. That is so utterly impossible you can't imagine.

CHRISTA. You can't be friends with her.

ALAN. It's not my choice.

CHRISTA. But you used to be close…

ALAN. Incredibly so.

CHRISTA. What happened?

*(**ALAN** places his hands on **CHRISTA**'s shoulders.)*

ALAN. I am not going to answer that right now. Right now I am going to put my hands on your shoulders. And keep them there. And I am going to let go when I feel I am able to. Okay?

CHRISTA. Okay.

(a beat)

ALAN. I like your shirt

CHRISTA. Annie says it makes my breasts look like beefsteak tomatoes

ALAN. She meant it as a compliment

CHRISTA. Of course.

(a beat)

ALAN. I like your smell.

CHRISTA. Shampoo. Annie's. I ran out.

ALAN. Of course.

*(**ALAN** kisses her deeply.)*

CHRISTA. Please.

ALAN. Leave

CHRISTA. Okay.

(She doesn't. **ALAN** *begins kissing her neck.)*

CHRISTA. Is there somewhere we can/

ALAN. Yes

CHRISTA. Will this be the last/

ALAN. Yes

CHRISTA. Then.

*(***ALAN*** scoops her up and carries her off.)*

(Lights up on **ANIMA** *sitting in a chair facing front, light of a video screen shining in her face, the tower of video tapes by her side.)*

*(***MOM*** and* **ARTIE** *appear, housecoated and diapered respectively.)*

MOM. What are you doing dear, don't you have class

ANIMA. It's Saturday, Ma

MOM. That's no excuse, you haven't been going to class at all, I know, a mother knows things, why are you at this place

ANIMA. Never mind, Ma

MOM. You don't know anything about video, Artie's the technical one, Artie should be in that chair playing with those knobs, you'd like that wouldn't you Artie

ARTIE. Yeah

MOM. Did you hear Annie, your brother Artemis was promoted to supervisor, isn't that wonderful, now he gets to wear a shirt and tie instead of a greasy uniform, isn't that right Artie

ARTIE. Yeah

MOM. It's about time, I mean after seven years Roy Rogers himself should have given Artie his tie.

(The tape stops forwarding and **CHRISTA**'s *voice is heard again, along with another woman's laughter.)*

CHRISTA. *(V.O.)* Now you push that – okay…it's a week before Christmas and my mom is wasted, I've never seen her drunk before, she's so funny

ANIMA. *(overlapping* **CHRISTA***'s voice)* There she is, Ma, she's laughing, when she laughs it's like a whole ocean opens up on you…

MOM. She's lovely, sweetie. No wonder you want to sleep with her

ANIMA. It's not that! It's, I don't know, it's not rational, my reason is fizzling away before me like the bubbles in a soda gone flat and I don't fucking care, mom, do you understand

MOM. Of course, sweetie. I felt the same way about Daddy once, before he turned into an abusive psychotic master of misery

ARTIE. Mom

MOM. Oh look, now you've upset Artie, he's gone and pooped his pants, you shouldn't say such things about your father Annie

ANIMA. I didn't/

MOM. He loved you very very much and broke his poor back to provide for his family, he just had trouble expressing his emotions, well we'd better get Artie home to change before he gets a rash, take care of yourself my darling girl, and please go to class, it's what Daddy would have wanted, let's go Artie.

(They vanish. **ANIMA** *stares ahead for a few moments.)*

ANIMA. It's a laugh that fills you like an ocean, the smooth way her skirt moves between her legs, the elegant column of smoke that rises from her lips when she drags from my cigarette, the sound of her coughing lightly in the next room, the way she sighs quietly sometimes when she eats, the slow burn of her features as I drift off to sleep

It's not about sex. It's not.

(Lights up on the apartment. **SUSAN** *has lost yet another leaf and is beginning to droop to one side. The video tapes are missing from the corner.)*

*(***CHRISTA*** *enters. Her hair is disheveled and there are dirt stains on her ass and knees.)*

(She drops her backpack on the ground and surveys the apartment. She walks over to the sickly **SUSAN**.*)*

CHRISTA. What's wrong, sweetie? You have the flu? A little pneumonia?

(She notices the blood. She touches it.)

The fuck is this...

*(***ANIMA*** *enters.)*

ANIMA. Hey

CHRISTA. Annie, take a look at this...what do you suppose that is....

ANIMA. Blood

CHRISTA. No, really

ANIMA. Blood

CHRISTA. Why would there be blood on the plant

ANIMA. I was feeding her

CHRISTA. What are you talking about

ANIMA. She looked sick. I thought she could use some iron

(a beat)

CHRISTA. You're serious.

ANIMA. It is my blood. I was feeding her my blood.

CHRISTA. You picked off your scab and fed her.

ANIMA. Yes.

CHRISTA. That's wrong, Annie, and weird.

ANIMA. I have plenty. Look at her. She's dying. Plants need iron, the fuck do you think they put in those plant pellets?

CHRISTA. Could you maybe not do it anymore?

ANIMA. If it's helping her what difference does it make

    (a beat)

    Are you busy right now?

CHRISTA. Sorta, why?

ANIMA. Let's go

CHRISTA. Where

ANIMA. It's a surprise

CHRISTA. Annie, I'm too tired

ANIMA. I have something planned

CHRISTA. You always do this, you act like I'm perpetually available to you

ANIMA. Aren't you

CHRISTA. I won't be someday

ANIMA. And when that day comes I shall drink Chlorox and set fire to my ass hair. But until then/

CHRISTA. You have ass hair?

ANIMA. UNTIL THEN, I will assume you are amenable to whatever delightful endeavor I fastidiously orchestrate for you

CHRISTA. Does it cost money

ANIMA. No

CHRISTA. Will it take long

ANIMA. No

CHRISTA. Should I bring my camcorder

ANIMA. No. Come on.

    *(She notices **CHRISTA**'s messy attire. She gestures to it.)*

ANIMA. Your new clothes.

CHRISTA. I tripped getting off the bus

ANIMA. Are you hurt

CHRISTA. Just my dignity…I'll just change…

ANIMA. I'm trying to figure out why you'd lie to me about this

CHRISTA. What makes you think I'm lying

ANIMA. You have a condom wrapper stuck to your ass

(**CHRISTA** *feels her ass. Indeed, she has a wrapper stuck there. She peels it off and crumples it up.*)

(*a beat*)

ANIMA. And the other night?

(**CHRISTA** *nods.*)

In the dirt. My pristine little roommie.

(*a beat*)

Was it fun?

(**CHRISTA** *is quiet.*)

Someone in your cohort?

CHRISTA. No

ANIMA. Someone you met at the bar

CHRISTA. No

ANIMA. Why won't you tell me

CHRISTA. Because I don't want to talk about it.

ANIMA. Oh. Okay.

(*a beat*)

CHRISTA. I should change.

(**CHRISTA** *starts toward her room and notices her stack of tapes is gone.*)

CHRISTA. Where are my tapes

ANIMA. I took them.

CHRISTA. You took my tapes?

ANIMA. I took your tapes.

CHRISTA. Why?

ANIMA. I can't tell you.

CHRISTA. Why did you take my tapes, Annie? It's a simple fucking question...

ANIMA. I just borrowed them/

CHRISTA. What the fuck is wrong with you, those are not your tapes, those are mine, my tapes, I told you I'd watch them with you, why the fuck couldn't you wait, what is wrong with you? Annie? What is wrong with you?

ANIMA. I…

CHRISTA. What?

(**ANIMA** *begins to curl into a fetal position and wheeze.*)

Wonderful…curl up and wheeze, great. That solves everything. Way to handle a situation with maturity and grace.

(**CHRISTA** *storms into her bedroom. After a moment she comes back out with her camcorder and begins filming* **ANIMA.**)

CHRISTA. This is my roommate Camera, in a rare display of self-indulgence and hyper-drama. She is the very picture of a modern American female enthralled by her own…histrionics…I'm sorry…

(**ANIMA** *continues to wheeze.* **CHRISTA** *lowers her camcorder and crouches by* **ANIMA**'s *side. She strokes* **ANIMA**'s *hair until* **ANIMA** *stops wheezing.*)

(*a beat*)

ANIMA. You stroke my hair like you love me.

CHRISTA. I do.

ANIMA. We're growing apart, Chris.

CHRISTA. We're not

ANIMA. I don't know why it's happening.

CHRISTA. We're NOT. Okay?

ANIMA. I'm scared.

(**CHRISTA** *puts her arms around* **ANIMA.**)

CHRISTA. (*french accent*) Mademoiselle. I am shocked and disappointed to see you have so little confidence in our, how you say…friendship.

(**ANIMA** *giggles.*)

I am afraid I will have to drown my sorrows in copious amounts of cheap wine. Care to join me?

ANIMA. Bien sur.

CHRISTA. And après, shall you take me to my surprise?

ANIMA. Oui.

CHRISTA. Then. I shall be but une moment.

*(**CHRISTA** disappears into her bedroom again. **ANIMA** picks up **CHRISTA**'s camcorder. She places it in the corner. She regards it.)*

*(Lights up on **CHRISTA** sitting in a movie chair. She is clutching a bottle of wine and taking huge gulps from it.)*

*(**ANIMA** is heard shouting from off.)*

ANIMA. *(offstage)* Is it blurry

CHRISTA. I can't tell, it's just a test pattern

ANIMA. *(offstage)* Is it blurry Chris?

CHRISTA. I said I can't tell…everything's a little blurry right now

ANIMA. *(offstage)* What?

CHRISTA. It's fine…

*(**CHRISTA** drinks. After a moment, **ANIMA** joins her.)*

ANIMA. Okay, now don't expect too much, I took editing last semester as a joke…the sound isn't exactly clean/

CHRISTA. Shhh….

("Smiling Face" is heard. A huge grin blooms on **CHRISTA**'s face.)*

Oh my god! Annie, what the fuck?

ANIMA. Mostly I just took clips you were in, ones where you were dancing or laughing…

CHRISTA. Oh my god!!!

*(**CHRISTA** laughs hysterically, then stops.)*

CHRISTA. Oh no I HATE that dress…I look like fucking Holly Hobby…

ANIMA. You DO! Wait wait, this is my favorite part…

(A beat. They both squeal in laughter, rolling around, out of breath.)

CHRISTA. Look at my HAIR…how could anyone let me walk around like that?

*See MUSIC USE note on page 3

ANIMA. I didn't know you then.

(*A beat as they watch.*)

CHRISTA. Annie, this...it's amazing.

ANIMA. Really really?

CHRISTA. Fucking YES!

(*She hugs* ANIMA *hard and long.*)

Thank you.

(*They continue watching the video.* CHRISTA *hands* ANIMA *the bottle of wine.* ANIMA *does not drink. Every now and then* CHRISTA *will exclaim "look at me" or "oh NO" or the like, laughing and shaking her head, or grabbing* ANIMA *in a side hug. This goes on a while, as* ANIMA *grows quiet and distant, and fidgety.*)

(*after long LONG beat*)

ANIMA. Do you love him, Chris?

(*a beat*)

CHRISTA. I barely know him.

ANIMA. Wow.

CHRISTA. What "wow"?

ANIMA. Nothing.

(*a beat*)

ANIMA. That's kinda messed up, is all.

CHRISTA. Why

ANIMA. You should have someone whose face you hold in your hands for hours after because you can't believe they exist. Not someone who throws you in the dirt and fucks up your new clothes

CHRISTA. It wasn't like that.

ANIMA. It's not worthy of you.

CHRISTA. "Worthy?" Give me a break

ANIMA. I am serious

CHRISTA. How do you justify it for yourself?

ANIMA. Justify what

CHRISTA. Sleeping with people you don't love.

ANIMA. I never have.

CHRISTA. That's such a lie.

ANIMA. It isn't.

CHRISTA. You're always talking about fucking, about wanting to fuck...

ANIMA. I do. Want to. I'd love to be able to mosey on into O'Briens, sidle up to some willowy young undergrad, drag him home by his sideburns and rodeo until dawn. But when it comes down to it, when bodies are involved, I just...something inside me stops.

CHRISTA. What about Alan?

(a beat)

You didn't love him, right?

(a beat)

I mean, you weren't IN love with him.

(a beat)

ANIMA. He never knew. We were friends for so long before, I was terrified. It was so bad, Chris. He'd sit next to me in class and you know people would be talking around us but I'd be totally zoned out, just inhaling him the whole time. He had such a particular smell. A mixture of like, lentil soup and scented toilet paper. And sometimes he'd call me really late and we'd talk until one of us fell asleep. He always passed out first. I'd listen to him breathing for a while, and then I'd say, "Alan. Alan. Hang up the phone." And sometimes he heard me and he'd hang up. But sometimes he didn't. So I'd just keep listening.

(a beat)

Whatever.

(A beat. They watch the video.)

It's almost over. I ran out of patience towards the end. Think I just let the last tape record straight through.

It's a good one, though. Looks like some college frat party. You have so much make-up on I barely recognized you.

(a beat)

CHRISTA. Annie…Why did you do this for me?

ANIMA. What do you mean?

CHRISTA. You took my tapes, you sat here for hours, you paid money you don't have to rent this equipment, it's not my birthday, so I'm just curious why you did this.

ANIMA. I…because…

*(A long beat. **ANIMA** leans over and kisses **CHRISTA** on the mouth softly. **CHRISTA** does not pull away.)*

ANIMA. Uh/

CHRISTA. Jesus/

ANIMA. Can't believe I just did that/

CHRISTA. Neither can I/

ANIMA. I never, I didn't want/

CHRISTA. It's okay, we've been drinking/

ANIMA. I want to do it again.

(a beat)

CHRISTA. Oh.

(a beat)

ANIMA. Okay

*(**ANIMA** stands to leave.)*

CHRISTA. Sit.

*(**ANIMA** shakes her head.)*

CHRISTA. Fucking sit, Annie.

*(**ANIMA** sits.)*

CHRISTA. You will not freak out about this, understand

*(**ANIMA** nods.)*

CHRISTA. We will finish watching your video, we will take the bus home, we will drag our drunk asses/ into bed

ANIMA. Why don't you want to kiss me?

CHRISTA. Oh Annie/

ANIMA. It doesn't mean anything, we can kiss and it doesn't have to fucking mean anything

CHRISTA. Calm down/

(**ANIMA** *tries to kiss* **CHRISTA** *again, more forcefully.* **CHRISTA** *pushes her away.* **ANIMA** *is crying.*)

CHRISTA. For fuck's sake!

ANIMA. You'll fuck some total stranger but you won't kiss me

CHRISTA. Goddamn it Annie, will you calm down

ANIMA. I can't stay here

(**ANIMA** *stands again and starts to exit, sobbing.*)

CHRISTA. SIT

ANIMA. I'm sorry, I'm so fucking sorry...

(**ANIMA** *exits.* **CHRISTA** *stares after her. a beat*)

CHRISTA. Okay.

(*Lights up on* **ANIMA**. *She is sitting on the couch, holding her knees and rocking.* **MARY-ANDROGYNE** *gazes at her in disapproval. The angels strum and hum their song.*)

MARY-ANDROGYNE. It's over, kitten...can't take a kiss back...

ANIMA. Where would she go...

MARY-ANDROGYNE. You want some answers? Watch her tape. The one in the camcorder

ANIMA. No

MARY-ANDROGYNE. She's laid it out for you, darling...the map of her passions...all you gotta do is press play...

ANIMA. It's wrong...

MARY-ANDROGYNE. You thought you knew her. Find out the truth. Watch the tape.

ANIMA. No.

MARY-ANDROGYNE. Watch the tape, darling.

ANIMA. Shut up

MARY-ANDROGYNE. Watch the tape watch the tape watch the tape watch the tape watch the tape /

(ANIMA takes a swing at MARY-ANDROGYNE's jaw. MARY-ANDROGYNE falls. The angels stop playing their music abruptly and rush to her side.)

ANIMA. You wouldn't stop/

MARY-ANDROGYNE. You just clocked the Virgin Mary

ANIMA. I'm sorry

MARY-ANDROGYNE. Do you know what happens when you clock the virgin Mary?

ANIMA. I don't

MARY-ANDROGYNE. *(sadly)* She bleeds from her broken heart until she dies.

(MARY-ANDROGYNE falls to the floor.. The angels vanish. MARY-ANDROGYNE sits up quickly and hands ANIMA the camcorder, then falls to the floor again.)

(After a moment's hesitation, she peers into the viewer of the camcorder and watches.)

(Lights up on ALAN in his apartment. He is sitting on his couch in his underwear, holding a woman's lighter and staring at it. Two half-empty glasses of wine sit on his coffee table. There is a light knock on his door.)

ALAN. Hang on

(He puts a bathrobe on and answers the door. It is CHRISTA. She stumbles in.)

Hi...

CHRISTA. Did I wake you

ALAN. No

CHRISTA. I'm sorry it's so fucking late

ALAN. Christ, you can barely walk

CHRISTA. I've been drinking

ALAN. I gathered

CHRISTA. I need another

ALAN. I don't think you do

CHRISTA. Please make me a fucking drink

ALAN. No

CHRISTA. Then I'll just take one of these

(**CHRISTA** *grabs one of the glasses of wine off the table.*)

ALAN. You are a mess

CHRISTA. I can't go home. I have no where else to go

ALAN. Did something happen

CHRISTA. Yes.

ALAN. With Annie?

CHRISTA. Yes. I think she went home. I can't go there.

ALAN. Did you have a fight?

CHRISTA. I just need to sit here for a second

ALAN. Do you want some water

CHRISTA. I just need to sit.

(**CHRISTA** *sits.*)

ALAN. It's good to see you.

CHRISTA. Thank you.

(**CHRISTA** *calms herself and looks around the apartment.*)

So this is what you wake up to every day

ALAN. Generally.

CHRISTA. It's not at all how I pictured

ALAN. How did you picture it

CHRISTA. Smaller. Spartan. One desk for your computer, mattress on the floor, milk crate furniture...

ALAN. It's not my stuff. I mean I didn't buy any of it

CHRISTA. Who did?

ALAN. Brenda. The woman I lived with for seven years. She left it as sort of severance pay for her lack of emotion on her departure

CHRISTA. Seven years. You were practically married.

ALAN. And of those wedded years, two were absolute bliss.

CHRISTA. Doesn't it break your heart to look at her things?

ALAN. Yes.

(a beat)

So what happened?

CHRISTA. God, where do I start?

*(**CHRISTA** takes out a pack of cigarettes.)*

Got a light?

ALAN. Annie's cigarettes.

CHRISTA. I bought these myself.

ALAN. Those are the brand she smokes.

CHRISTA. Oh.

*(**ALAN** hands her the woman's lighter. **CHRISTA** lights her cigarette and inspects the lighter.)*

Quite a girly lighter for such a manful young stag

ALAN. Not mine either

CHRISTA. Brenda's?

ALAN. No

CHRISTA. Whose

ALAN. A friend's

(a beat)

CHRISTA. Oh.

*(**CHRISTA** looks at the glasses of wine.)*

Oh my God, I'm so stupid…She was here tonight. I'm drinking her wine, aren't I?

ALAN. Yes.

CHRISTA. *(a whisper)* Is she still here?

ALAN. No.

CHRISTA. Is it someone you've been seeing

ALAN. No. I picked her up in a bar in Hollywood.

CHRISTA. Do you do that often

ALAN. No

CHRISTA. Well. Congrats on your conquest. Must be hard for you to keep track of all the ladies that touch your dick every day

(**CHRISTA** *stands to leave.*)

ALAN. I didn't sleep with her/

CHRISTA. I'm such an idiot/

ALAN. I did not sleep with her.

(**CHRISTA** *is frantically, drunkenly trying to leave. He stops her.*)

I brought her home because I kept thinking of you and I wanted to stop.

CHRISTA. Why?

ALAN. Why do you think?

(*a beat*)

CHRISTA. This is so fucked up…

(*She gets up to leave.*)

ALAN. Christa. You are too drunk. Stay.

CHRISTA. I'm not staying here.

ALAN. You're not thinking straight / right now

CHRISTA. I AM NOT STAYING / IN THIS

ALAN. Right, and you can't go HOME, because of some, uh, enigmatic cataclysm, so what, you're gonna find a box under the 405, go hang out in Volunteer Park, what/ is your

CHRISTA. STOP, JUST…EVERYTHING, STOP.

(*A beat.* **ALAN** *shakes his head.*)

ALAN. I literally cannot BELIEVE what I'm seeing here. It's like a, a seven car pile up at the bottom of an icy hill. It's…

CHRISTA. It's a WHAT?

ALAN. It's not you, Christa. I mean, what little I know of you. It's someone else. Not you.

CHRISTA. *(quietly)* Histrionics. My specialty.

(A beat. He touches her face.)

ALAN. Chris…

CHRISTA. I have many, MANY things to think about right now…but I can't do a good job at it while you're doing that…so. Okay.

(She pulls away. A beat. She grabs the last of the wine and downs it.)

ALAN. I, I'm not sure how to make this easier for either of us…but I think we should/ try to figure

CHRISTA. Some, some damage control, a little…Yeah. I'm going home now. Everything will be fine.

ALAN. Christa.

CHRISTA. Goodbye.

> *(**CHRISTA** exits. **ALAN** fondles the glass she drank from. She returns a second later and kisses him passionately and sloppily, then stumbles out the door.)*
>
> *(Lights up on the apartment. **MARY-ANDROGYNE** is lying on the floor dead. Her exposed heart is bleeding.)*
>
> *(**ANIMA** is sitting in the dark. **CHRISTA** stumbles in, holding a bottle of Jack and smoking.)*

CHRISTA. Hi.

ANIMA. Hi.

> *(a beat)*

CHRISTA. Wanna talk?

ANIMA. Yes.

> *(**CHRISTA** goes to turn the lights on.)*

Please. Leave them off.

CHRISTA. Okay.

> *(a beat)*

Are you trashed too?

ANIMA. I am completely sober.

CHRISTA. Wow.

 (a beat)

 Do you want to start or should I?

ANIMA. I think maybe. I should.

CHRISTA. Okay.

 (a beat)

ANIMA. I have a question.

CHRISTA. Okay.

ANIMA. Those women you study, the ones who were trying to trash their identities and find new ones…Did they do it?

CHRISTA. That's an odd question…

ANIMA. Did they?

CHRISTA. No. They created a new model.

ANIMA. How

CHRISTA. By combining qualities of both worlds.

ANIMA. You know the difference between you and them?

 (a beat)

 They had fucking chops.

CHRISTA. Am I supposed to know what that means?

 (a beat)

 Because I wouldn't kiss you?

 (a beat)

 I don't understand what is going on here, Annie.

ANIMA. I watched your tape. The one in the camcorder.

CHRISTA. When.

ANIMA. About an hour ago.

CHRISTA. Unbelievable.

 (a beat)

 Something was on it. Something that upset you.

ANIMA. You don't remember.

 (a beat)

CHRISTA. Oh my god....

ANIMA. No.

CHRISTA. Oh Annie...

ANIMA. No. No. Don't do that right now.

CHRISTA. What...what....

> (**ANIMA** *grabs* **CHRISTA**'s *hands tightly. She remains calm and speaks slowly.*)

ANIMA. Stop. Okay? Calmly. "We were drunk, Annie."

CHRISTA. Annie...

ANIMA. "We were drunk, Annie."

CHRISTA. We were drunk, Annie.

ANIMA. "Both times, Annie."

> (*A beat.* **CHRISTA** *shakes her head no.* **ANIMA** *lets out a small noise, as if she is being punched. She regains composure and does not let go of* **CHRISTA**'s *hands.*)

ANIMA. Okay. "I went to his place tonight, Annie."

CHRISTA. I went to his place tonight, Annie.

ANIMA. "To talk to him. About you."

CHRISTA. No.

ANIMA. "I am falling in love with him, Annie/"

CHRISTA. No, Annie, no...

ANIMA. Shhh...I need you to say it. Even if it isn't true. Please.

> (*a beat*)

CHRISTA. I am falling in love with him, Annie.

> (**ANIMA** *lets out another small noise. She doesn't let go of* **CHRISTA**'s *hands. She is possibly about to begin wheezing but breathes deeply and stops herself.*)

> (*a beat*)

ANIMA. Okay. Okay. I'm okay. One more. "I didn't know you were in love with him until tonight, Annie."

CHRISTA. I didn't

ANIMA. "I didn't know, Annie"

CHRISTA. I didn't. I didn't.

ANIMA. Okay.

> *(a beat)*

> Okay.

> *(They sit in silence for a few moments, holding hands.)*

ANIMA. This is us, Christa. It's happening.

CHRISTA. It's not what I want. Not ever, not ever.

ANIMA. I've been sitting on this couch for hours thinking of your mouth – don't pull away. Your mouth. Moving. And your hair. Trying to conjure the correct version of you so I could see this all with some sort of precision. But you kept blurring. Even now. Your hands. They feel like I could press just a little harder and your bones would crush into dust beneath your skin. But I know they are the same hands as before.

> I know they are. Okay Christa? I *know* it. But I still fucking hate you right now.

> *(a beat)*

> Right now.

> *(**ANIMA** stands and walks over to **SUSAN**, who is completely stripped of leaves and looking quite sickly. She begins to drag her to the front door.)*

CHRISTA. Where, where/ are you

ANIMA. I need to do this. Okay.

> *(**ANIMA** exits with **SUSAN**.)*

> *(A moment. **CHRISTA** curls up and beings to wheeze, but stops herself. She sits up and looks around the room. Slowly, methodically, she begins to tidy up.)*

> *(Lights on **ANIMA**, perched on the edge of the stage, her pants rolled up and her feet bare. She is scooping the ocean into her hands and cleaning **SUSAN**'s leaves. Her hair is blowing in the sea air.)*

> *(**MOM** and **ARTIE** appear.)*

ARTIE. The long green sea on your tongue

MOM. The long green sea in your hair

ARTIE. Between your toes

MOM. A million ancient stars between your toes

ARTIE. A million miles of sea on your tongue

MOM. A million miles

ARTIE. Salt and sky to fill your cells

MOM. Fill your eyes

ARTIE. In your cut before the scab

MOM. A million miles.

(**ANIMA** *speaks to* **SUSAN.**)

ANIMA. This is the ocean, Susan. She's vast, isn't she? The yellow afternoon hanging low above her is her father. He dreamed of her once filled with jewels, emeralds and sapphires and diamonds, and she stayed that way. She winks and twinkles for a million miles.

You've probably dreamed her as well. Remember the ache you felt in your stem, the small half-pains, the yawning itch...it was her voice riding your dream tides. Stretch to her, Susan. Let each new leaf uncurl one by one like fingers in a fist and let your palms be tickled by her green breath.

(**ANIMA** *stretches to the ocean.*)

See? It's easy. Try. That's it.

(**ANIMA** *continues to stretch.*)

MOM. Now that you're here Annie, what shall you do

ANIMA. (*to* **SUSAN**) Stretch

ARTIE. Now that you're here Annie, what shall you do

ANIMA. Stretch

MOM. What shall you do, Annie

ANIMA. Stretch. Stretch.

(*After a moment,* **ARTIE** *and* **MOM** *begin to stretch toward the ocean.*)

ANIMA. That's it. Good girl.

(*Lights slowly fade.*)

End of Play

Also by
Sheila Callaghan...

Ayravana Flies, or A Pretty Dish

Crawl, Fade to White

Dead City

We Are Not These Hands

That Pretty Pretty; or, The Rape Play

Please visit our website **samuelfrench.com** for complete
descriptions and licensing information

From the Reviews of
SCAB...

"Brilliantly and poetically rendered...[Callaghan's] playful sense of language and her attunement to her characters are enthralling." – *Time Out Chicago*

"*Scab*...is a textbook example of promising work, written with a yen for interesting language and liberally salted with well-observed details of the lives of newly minted adults...the play shines." – *The New York Times*

"Darkly funny forays into the surreal...Callaghan shows talent in the inventive fantasy sequences...
A stylish production."
– *The Village Voice*

CPSIA information can be obtained
at www.ICGtesting.com
Printed in the USA
BVHW02s2150041117
499557BV00017B/286/P